PROFESSIONALING
IS HARD

I0620500

22 LESSONS TO HELP MAKE IT
(A LITTLE) EASIER

Kristin Fahy

For permission requests, write to the publisher, at the following email address:
kristin@impetushealthllc.com

Ordering Information:
Quantity sales. Special discounts are available on quantity purchases by corporations, associations, and others. For details, contact the publisher at the following email address:
kristin@impetushealthllc.com

Library of Congress Control Number: 2023921713

Professionaling Is Hard/ Kristin Fahy. —1st ed.
ISBN 979-8-218-31838-3

Photo by: Ericka Kreutz

For you, may even one thing you read here make something easier to navigate.

And for my best girl, my star, and my awesome – may all your professional dreams come true someday.

Professionaling Is Hard

CONTENTS

Ugh?! Why did it have to be so hard, and why did it take me so long to figure this out? There have been so many times in my career when I've exhaustedly found myself saying that after I learned what, in hindsight, seemed like an obvious lesson. I just wish it had been any easier or that someone had given me a playbook for how to handle things at work.

This book is intended to be that for you. It's the collection of lessons I wish someone had handed me during the first several years of my career when I was overcoming personal obstacles and stepping on interpersonal landmines. During those years, I was starving for guidance and mentorship and had no idea where to find it. Navigating the professional world around me felt lonely and scary at best. I only wish I'd bought shares in Ben and Jerry's so I might have gotten a return on all the late-night consoling I did with them.

I've always had a flair for needing to learn things on my own and in my own time. So, I'll be the first to admit that if someone had handed me a book of professional lessons back then, I'm not sure I would have accepted it at first. Yet what I've learned since then is that I can't possibly live long enough to make every mistake and always know how to handle things. It's far more efficient for me to listen to advice from the people who've already made the mistakes, acquired the lessons, and worked their way to where they want to be. There is a lot of wisdom in their trials and tribulations that helps me find my way.

What follows in this book are 22 lessons from my own gauntlet of professional experiences. Each one shares personal stories about how I learned that lesson and at times I share tricks and tools that have helped me since. I close each one out with a question or two for you to consider about how that lesson may apply in your own professional world.

The book is divided into three sections. The first section is a series of lessons that are more personally focused on how to manage ourselves better. The second section is all about interpersonal dynamics at work and how to help navigate them. The last section presents a series of lessons that seem oppositional at first, but upon further review present a more well-rounded view of the options that may be available to us in a given situation. This section also covers a range of both personal as well as more interpersonal lessons.

I hope you enjoy reading these lessons as much as I enjoyed writing them. I tried to offer as much insight as I could and share as many practical application tips as possible to help you on your own journey.

It is often said that there is no substitute for experience but my hope in sharing these lessons is that you can add years of wisdom to your knowledge base and have practical tools to turn back to time and again. I hope this saves you from some of my mistakes and sets you further down a path blazing whatever trail you choose. May all your professionaling be easier from here!

Professionaling Is Hard

Section One: The Personal

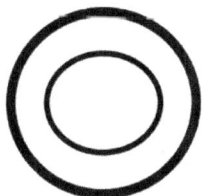

The first series of lessons is all about building and reinforcing inner strength. It is a series of things that, once realized, can help you:

- Get up learning curves more quickly.
- Make decisions faster and with less pressure.
- Find a starting place when you're stuck.
- Manage expectations and look good doing it.
- Feel confident about what you bring to the table.

LESSON ONE:

NO ONE EXPECTS YOU TO HAVE IT ALL FIGURED OUT

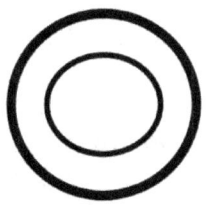

*You don't have to know everything on day one,
you just need to show you can figure it out.*

Lesson One

Yikes, the pressure I placed upon myself to know everything before my hand even touched the front door on day one of my first professional job is daunting even when I think about it now. I was so scared that they would discover how little I actually knew and how very much I was maybe not the best person for this role. Imposter syndrome is something I dabbled in quite liberally. If I'm honest, I still have to manage that; it's a very real thing.

Looking back, I'm amazed at how much pressure I put on myself to know things I could never have known and how very little all of that mattered once I got into the work itself. What ultimately did matter was that I had a willingness to figure things out. I'm scrappy and independent. I try to get answers and do things on my own as quickly and efficiently as I can, so I don't have to "bother" people to explain things to me. However, as I learned in one early position, spinning my wheels instead of asking someone for help isn't the best approach.

When I was in a new role that required me to get familiar with a lot of very strict policies and protocols, the number of things to know and places to look for information seemed endless. It was daunting, and we had a very small staff, so I didn't want to annoy anyone with questions. I threw myself into it and tried to figure out how exactly to figure things out... on my own. My boss noticed, and I felt proud that she could see I was working hard and doing all I could to learn and get up to speed.

Yet after a few weeks of this, despite all my efforts, it still wasn't coming together. I felt insecure and embarrassed to ask for help. I didn't want to look like I didn't know things. Then during a one-on-one, my boss asked me about a few of the things I just couldn't seem to figure out no matter how hard I tried. It quickly illuminated the gaps in my understanding. She seemed frustrated. My blind spots became apparent, as did the amount of time I was spending on them at the cost of not learning more things.

As much as it pained and humiliated me, she told me I needed to get better at knowing when to ask for help. Ugh. Icky. Ask for help?! Yes, be resourceful and try to find answers, but if I'm spending more than a reasonable amount of time and coming up empty, I need to make a list and ask for help so I can learn it and move on. Ugh, fine, I'll ask for help when I need to. Benadryl® anyone?

With her guidance, it taught me to continually establish the line on when to ask for help many times over in new situations. Here are some things that help:

- Asking your manager for an estimate of how long they think something will take. Getting a benchmark from them and tracking against it can be a super helpful gauge.

- Ask your manager and/or colleagues if there are any tips, tricks, or tools they've used that have been effective. You never know when someone else has created a resource they might be willing to share.

- Trust your gut based on how long other related things have taken. I've found there's usually a pattern or a cadence to learning. If it generally takes 10-15 minutes on something similar but you've put in over 30 minutes on this, that might be a cue that you need to ask for help.

- When all else fails – google or go to AI. The vast number of resources at our fingertips compared to when I started out is staggering. If you can't find the answer in what you've been given, check there. Just be sure to be discerning about what you find and check with someone to confirm it.

Learning when I've exhausted a reasonable amount of time trying to figure something out on my own and when I need to ask for help has enabled me to get up learning curves more quickly. It has also deepened relationships with people by asking them for guidance as I go. People generally feel good about knowing things and having an opportunity to share their wisdom.

When starting out somewhere or beginning something new it's easy to feel an enormous amount of pressure to have all the answers. Ultimately, people don't expect us to know everything - they just expect us to be able to figure things out and learn to do so in an efficient way. Whether that's searching on our own, or asking someone for help, finding the right balance is what people expect us to be able to do quickly.

Questions to Consider:

Can you think of any examples of doing things on your own to avoid asking for help?

If you had received help more quickly, what might you have had more time to do?

Professionaling Is Hard

LESSON TWO:

THIS IS ONE CHOICE - NOT A LIFE SENTENCE

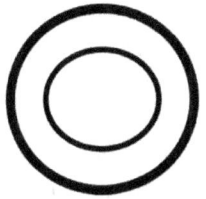

Don't put too much pressure on one decision
(in a lifetime of continually making new ones).

It is so easy to feel like the stakes for decisions like leaving a job for a new one are life or death. Yes, for most of us, we are absolutely dependent on earning a living in order to have shelter and provisions, so, in a sense, having a job is life or death. However, in reality, the gravity of deciding what to do next is oftentimes given far more weight than is helpful or practical. It's one decision in a lifetime of continually making new decisions because we can, and will, always need to decide more things.

I've done it more times than I can count. Spun out and become wildly anxious because something feels like it's a make-or-break decision. Do I take that opportunity, or do I stay here? What happens to me if I...? Will I be earning enough to....? What doors will be closed if I....? Where will I be in 10 years if I....? I spin and spin and spin. It winds up feeling like the weight of a thousand worlds is on top of me to make this one choice. I've spun too far, and I no longer have any objectivity or sense of what I want. I just need snacks and a nap.

Desperate for professional guidance in my late twenties I joined the Healthcare Businesswomen's Association (HBA). I quickly learned they had a mentoring program and I enthusiastically signed up. During one of our mentoring sessions when I wasn't personally in a spin cycle of doom, I heard our mentor give some sage advice to a fellow mentee who was very much in her own active spin.

The mentor acknowledged that it can feel intense to make a decision like the one the mentee was facing, but that ultimately, she would make many big decisions over the course of her lifetime, and this just happened to be the one on deck right now. No matter what she decided, this was not going to be the thing that kills her. It was not a tiger chasing her, and there would be another decision for her to make again soon. Plus, she could always decide something different later if she hated it. Life is about making decisions based on what's in front of you, and the only constant is change.

She also suggested that a good old pro-con list was a helpful way of getting the spin out of her mind and onto paper, to take a more objective look at things. This would also provide a record of what she had been thinking should she question the decision later and want to revisit why she chose what she did.

There have been so many times since then where I've recalled the wisdom of her words when I realized I was getting upset about a major decision. When you face those moments, it's helpful to:

- Go to the extreme and remind yourself that this is not a tiger chasing you. It instantly deescalates things and brings some levity to the situation.

- From there make a pro-con list and arrive at a more objective decision.

- Trust your gut. Once we're out of a panic state and have assessed things more objectively, it's much easier to check in with our gut instinct.

Life is nothing if not a series of decisions we need to navigate making. We're more powerful when we learn to make them from a place of remembering it is one of many and we can always make new ones.

Questions to Consider:

What's one decision you've faced that seemed really overwhelming and stressful to make at the time?

Looking back, how, if at all, could you have deescalated the pressure you felt?

If you make a pro-con list about a decision, does an answer seem clearer?

LESSON THREE:

BITE-SIZED

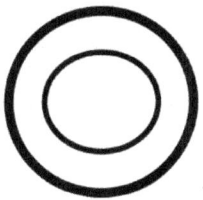

*Identifying and taking one tiny action can free
you from being stuck.*

Lesson Three

When things are stuck and not moving, the very best thing I've found that helps is to identify one tiny bite-sized thing I can do. By shifting my energy into doing one small thing, I get out of my head and into gear. It changes everything.

Despite being a highly motivated action-oriented person who wants to be doing at all times, there are moments or hours or even longer where I am completely stuck and fully spinning my wheels not going anywhere. I am in Stuckville, and I cannot for the life of me find a way out of town. Every road is a dead end and brings me right back to the fetal position on the couch, panic and anxiety drumming in my chest like the Blueman Group is in there.

Sometimes I'll call people moaning and groaning about all that's wrong looking for sympathy and oftentimes polling people to see what I should do. That, I can tell you, is not a winning strategy. While it does sometimes help to be heard, ultimately, I'm the only one who should be making these choices. I should not be outsourcing my decisions, and I definitely should not be looking for other people to make something okay for me to do; that's my job.

I've taken the CliftonStrengths® assessment twice over the years, and three of my top five strengths are strategy, ideation, and futuristic. Even if you're not familiar with the test (it's fun and useful, do it!), what this means is that I'm a lady who is very comfortable having her head in the clouds dreaming of how to create things, imagining the new, and optimizing how to bring it to life.

I share that because those strengths can also lead to a lot of paralysis. When you can imagine so many options and you've peered down the road of strategy enough to visualize how to best make things happen, it can leave you circling the drain and panicking about what to do next or how to get started. When you like living at 30,000 feet, it's really hard to find the one foot in front of you that matters.

It's in those moments, and from that place that I've come to find it invaluable to start by breaking it down, as much as is humanly possible, into very actionable bite-sized steps. When things seem so high stakes or like there are too many things to do or choose from, sometimes the best thing to do is just find a place to start with one tiny thing. Even if that thing gets tossed, it gets those doing muscles firing and moves me out of the clouds and into action.

Often once I've initiated something other things start to become clearer. I've engaged kinetic energy, and I find myself staying in motion and moving fluidly as the dots on what to do next begin to connect before me. It's been a huge tool in helping me get unstuck. This book is an example of this concept in action. My bite-sized thing was to write a couple of sentences about a lesson I'd learned. Four hours later when I stood up, I had written a large part of what's in this book.

If you're like me, you find it all too easy to spin and swirl and not know where to begin sometimes. That struggle is very real. Yet finding that one bite-sized thing that is possible to do is a game changer to breaking out of Stuckville and getting into motion.

Questions to Consider:

Is there one small thing you could do that you suspect would start a chain reaction?

Next time you find yourself getting stuck could you give yourself permission to pick a starting place to get things in motion?

LESSON FOUR:

UNDER-PROMISE, OVER-DELIVER

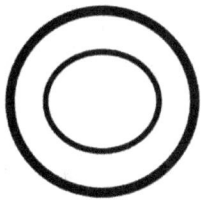

*Setting expectations so you can exceed them is
a good way to make a great impression.*

Lesson Four

I only wish I knew the concept of under-promise, over-deliver when I was an eager beaver first starting out in my career. This is back in the days when if someone said they wanted 60 hours of work done by tomorrow at noon – I would say, "sure, no problem!" What?! No. I got on the superhighway to crushing myself and disappointing others way too often. All-nighters, weekends, a lot of my time was spent doing an unrealistic amount of work in an unrealistic amount of time.

I cringe when I think of how the people-pleasing part of me that needed to prove myself wouldn't push back or set reasonable expectations. So, instead I would sell myself out and pay for it dearly. There was one period where I didn't have a day off for three months. There is no way I was producing my best work.

During one of these periods of setting unrealistic expectations, I got pinched. We had committed to way more than we should have, and I was on the hook for more than I could possibly get done in the amount of time we had. I thought I could pull all-nighters and make it all happen, but one thing after another hit snags, and I simply ran out of runway. I had to go to the client and ask for an extension on delivering something because I couldn't get it done in time. I was mortified. They weren't pleased because they had to reset expectations internally on their side. It ended up being fine, but that's not who I wanted to be or how I wanted to operate, to say nothing of how awful it felt, and how exhausted I was.

After that happened, a kinder soul in sales helped me begin to set better timelines and supported me in learning to push back when clients wanted things sooner or to expand scope without adjusting for it accordingly. It went against my grain to not "yes" people, but she helped me see that when you set expectations that give you enough room, people are thrilled if you can do more or deliver it ahead of time. Doing the opposite inevitably disappoints. Note: I'm referring to a client situation, but the same principle can be applied to any internal "client": boss, colleague, a different department, etc.

What helped me get better at under-promising and over-delivering was learning how to estimate my workload more effectively.

I started by looking at three variables to consider when estimating what we can get done:

- The quantity of work to be done.
- The amount of time to do it in.
- The quality of the work produced.

Here is a sample of the steps to walk through to help with estimating getting a body of work done:

- Break things up into tasks or actions that need to be done (e.g., research, analyze, report, summarize, edit, review).

- Estimate the amount of time it will likely take to complete each task or action. Using ranges can help to get a minimum and maximum amount of time (e.g., 6-8 hours for research).

- List the other things you're working on and consider how they impact your availability to do these tasks or actions.

- Build a timeline for how long you realistically think it will take you to complete all the tasks or actions you identified given all that's on your plate.

Consider going to the maximum side of the range and/or add in wiggle room for the inevitable delay or setback. You can always negotiate down but start with more time than you need.

As you begin, be sure to track your actual time to complete something against your estimate to see how close you were. Tracking your hours to see how long things are taking you will help you get better at estimating your time in the future.

Once we have a ballpark estimate for the amount of time it takes to get certain quantities of work done, we can consider other variables and adjust as needed. If something is urgent so you have less time, that likely means the amount that is produced, or the quality must also be adjusted down. If more work or higher quality work is desired, it's reasonable to think that will add time.

There's a concept in project management called the Iron Triangle. The three sides of the triangle are scope, time, and cost, with quality sitting in the middle. It's a helpful visual to assess the trade-offs between the three variables while keeping an eye on quality. I omitted cost here in my example, but if your job requires managing projects, it's worth reading more about this concept sometime.

It's life, things inevitably pop up that require unanticipated time and attention. Learning to estimate your workload and giving yourself reasonable timelines ensures that you can do your best work and provide the best results. Plus, if you can do it ahead of schedule or do more than what was promised - people are usually thrilled.

Whenever possible, under-promising and over-delivering is a great way to ensure expectations are not only met, but possibly even exceeded.

Question to Consider:

Are there any places where you might be able to reassess things to find opportunities to under-promise and over-deliver?

Professionaling Is Hard

LESSON FIVE:

BE CONFIDENT IN WHAT YOU KNOW

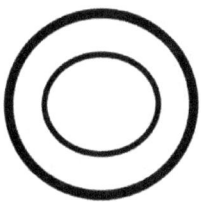

Remembering to focus on what we already know helps build confidence when the pressure is on.

Lesson Five

At high-stakes times such as job interviews or presenting to an intimidating group of people, it helps to remember you wouldn't be there if you hadn't earned your way through the door. Learning to take stock of who you are, what you've done, and what you know so you can hold your head high is an invaluable lesson.

I will never forget how terrified I was to present the findings from a qualitative primary market research study I had conducted to a group of around 20 people at the client's office. The audience would be senior leadership, scientists, smart people who knew things and had degrees I didn't even know existed.

I was somewhat new to the job, and this was my first major presentation to a client on my own. The company was at a pivotal point, the stakes for them were very high, and they were looking to this research to help them make some important decisions. No pressure.

My boss at the time knew I was sweating it. She was far from the kindest boss I ever had, but seeing the anxiety swelling in me as I prepared and did some practice runs with her, she gave me advice that has stuck with me ever since.

She told me to forget what the people I was presenting to were experts of and focus on what I was the expert of - the data. They didn't do the interviews, read the transcripts, analyze the data, or write the report like I did. I was the expert of all that, and that's all I needed to focus on. Sure, they might have questions, but my only job was to acknowledge what was in the data and nothing more.

It took the edge off feeling the pressure that I had to know everything about their business or that I might be the only person in that room without a PhD or MD in something I likely couldn't pronounce. I just needed to focus on what I already knew better than anyone else. I was an expert on what was in the report I wrote.

Whether it's presenting to a group, trying to land a job, networking, or life itself, one of the best lessons I've learned is to be confident in who I am and what I know. The same goes for you. No one else knows exactly what you know or has had the experiences you've had. All you need to do is be confident in yourself and trust that you'll navigate things the best that you can.

Questions to Consider:

Is there something you feel intimidated about at work?

Can you break it down into facts about what you already know, qualifications you already have, or transferable experiences or skills under your belt?

Section Two: The

Interpersonal

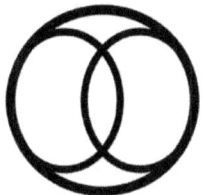

The second series of lessons is all about how to work with other people. This can be a slippery slope at times. It helps to have tips and tools in our back pocket when we find ourselves in sticky situations with others. This series of lessons will help you:

- Learn how to navigate making a mistake.

- Get (and give) specific examples to guide feedback.

- Confirm alignment and cover your bases.

- Be more direct and timelier with difficult conversations.

- Identify and manage discrepancies between someone's words and deeds.

- Be more objective and take things less personally.

- Find your voice and pass the mic to others.

LESSON SIX:

IT'S OKAY TO MAKE MISTAKES

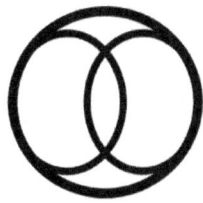

*Mistakes happen, report them quickly with
some thought towards possible solutions.*

Lesson Six

Show me the person who claims they've never made a mistake professionally, and I'll show you a liar. Not one person on this planet has done everything perfectly every single time. To err is human as they say. And yet I remember being absolutely terrified of making mistakes at work. It felt as if I'd be sent to the guillotine for misspelling something or forgetting to put something in its proper place.

There are two things I've found are important when dealing with mistakes:

- Report it as quickly as possible.
- Identify some possible solutions or remedies to the situation.

As a manager, there have been times when someone waited to tell me about a mistake until our standard weekly meeting instead of reporting it sooner. In some situations, that's created more problems because they addressed things, but in a way that caused more issues, so then we had a bigger situation on our hands.

Once, my boss came to me about a mistake they heard someone on my team had made that I was unaware of. It didn't look good for me or the person who made the mistake that I didn't know about it. If I had known, I could have supported my team member. Instead, hearing about it through the grapevine from other people's perspectives meant the mistake-maker lost control of the narrative. It took me by surprise hearing it from someone else, and it put a ding in the trust I thought we had established. No one likes to be caught off guard, especially the person who's supposed to have your back.

As an employee, I feel much better going to someone and alerting them to a problem or a mistake if I also come prepared with some thoughts on how it might be remedied. When they first hear about it, their mind will be racing to damage control, so I like to demonstrate that I've thought about that too and have some ideas for how to make things right. It shows responsibility and proactiveness even in the face of an error.

Mistakes happen to the best of us, and when they do, prompt acknowledgment of them matters to avoid additional damage. It's also helpful to begin thinking about how to remedy the situation. It's always easier to share, and receive bad news when possible solutions have been considered.

Questions to Consider:

Looking back on any mistakes or errors you've made, is there anything you would do differently?

When other people make mistakes that impact you, how do you want them to handle it with you?

LESSON SEVEN:

ASK FOR AN EXAMPLE

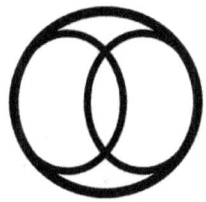

When feedback is general or not specific enough to be informative, ask for an example.

Lesson Seven

There have been times in my life when a manager or supervisor has criticized my work or given me harsh feedback. Some of those times, my work wasn't as good as it could have been, and the feedback, while hurtful, was ultimately helpful to my development. That is... once I had licked my wounds and was able to hear the merit of what they were saying. Other times what they were criticizing felt exaggerated, wrong, or inaccurate.

I fully and readily admit I am a sensitive person. In the past, I took what other people said as truth without question. If someone said my writing sucked, I took it to heart, felt hopeless, and tried to figure out what on earth I could possibly do to make up for my horrific flaw. I operated from a place of assuming everyone else knew better than I did. Anything but a position of confidence or power, yet in some cases, something would needle at me. I'm not that bad. I'm not an idiot. Somewhere deep down there was some feedback I knew I might not have wholly deserved.

One manager of mine could be particularly critical and had a reputation for finding something to critique you on and then continuing to hold it against you, even if you made great efforts and improved upon it. While the accusations and criticism stung and made me feel ashamed of my work, I knew the quality of what I produced well enough to know that some of what was being said was unfair or unwarranted. It was from that place that I finally got the gumption to begin asking for examples.

This became an invaluable tool for me when working with this person and in general. At times it's easy to generalize what someone does or to pick at something that's not how you might do it. Yet I realized that when I asked the person making critiques to take something from a general comment like "you're not being assertive enough" and give me a specific example of where I missed an opportunity to be more assertive, it helped us have a much more balanced and thorough conversation.

If there was an actual example, it would give me a real opportunity to examine things and evaluate what I could do differently that would be more in line with what was expected of me and what gaps I might need help closing to get there. If they couldn't produce an example, it was a good opportunity to talk about what was happening, and often, I ended up getting praised for the work I was doing.

As a manager, I've learned that when I notice someone has an opportunity to step up their game, it's more effective if I come prepared by referencing a specific example and asking them what they think about it. This way I get a baseline on their perceptions, and we can use that example as a starting place for the conversation. It's much more helpful and productive than speaking about something generally.

Things move quickly. It's easy to want more or different from people no matter what they're doing or how hard they're working. Learning to ask someone for an example when they're giving feedback that is general and not specific is a very powerful tool. It can help make things more concrete and actionable, and it can build alignment around something that initially seemed off-base.

Questions to Consider:

Is there any general feedback you've been given that you could go back and ask for specific examples about?

LESSON EIGHT:

GET IT IN WRITING

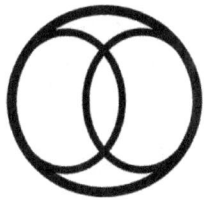

Get promises or commitments in writing to ensure there is a documented mutual understanding.

Lesson Eight

Some of the biggest professional regrets I have stem from this one. When I was growing up, my father used to lament about one of his friends who worked for someone who promised him up and down that when he retired, he'd "take care" of my father's friend. It drove my father nuts that his friend took the business owner at his word and didn't have anything in writing. It made him profoundly worried for his friend and was a sentiment that was eventually proven to be founded.

With that foundational cautionary tale in mind, you'd think that I would have avoided a similar fate, but unfortunately, not so.

The first time I was working like a dog for a company, grinding myself beyond what was reasonable, when someone reached out about a job opportunity at their company. It sounded interesting, and since I didn't feel like I was being treated well or appreciated where I was, I interviewed. I ended up getting an offer, but I also wasn't solidly convinced it was the right next step for me. I went to my employer, and the person in charge authorized a counteroffer increasing my salary and committing to a title change and further bump in pay at my next review about 5 months out. I decided to stay where I was and kept working away diligently.

When my review came up, I thoroughly expected things to go as promised. When I saw my boss's face as we sat down, I knew something was wrong. He said that the person in charge, my boss's boss, said I was never promised a promotion and raise. My heart sank. He looked me in the eyes and made that offer to get me to stay, but I should have gotten it in writing. Needless to say, it wasn't long after that I did find a new opportunity and left, but it stung that I failed to get it in writing in the first place.

The second time I was helping someone start a company. I was taking a big hit financially to focus on exploring this new venture, so the person I was working with and I agreed there was meaningful opportunity cost to be rewarded if things worked out. Sweat equity. We agreed the investment I was making to get this company off the ground was foundational, and I was promised up and down that I'd be taken care of when the time came, just trust. That went on and on for years. When the time finally came to put together an agreement honoring my contribution, it became very clear that our estimations of the value of my investment were worlds apart. I was devastated. I should have known better.

I'm embarrassed that I didn't value myself enough to push for more of an understanding of how my contribution would be estimated. In both situations, I didn't want to "make them mad" or "push too hard," afraid that they would give me less. I wish I had had the courage to honor and value myself enough to get something in writing, so I knew where I stood, and my bases were covered. I let myself down.

If I could go back, I would be firmer and more confident in asking for what was promised in writing. If someone wasn't willing to do so, I should have identified it as a red flag and been prepared to pursue other options.

When the stakes are high or when things are promised to you, it's important to get it in writing. This way nothing is murky. There is an undeniable trail of what was agreed upon, and all parties have the freedom to operate from a place of mutual respect and understanding.

Question to Consider:

If there is any ambiguity about anything in your professional world, can you ask for clarity and get it in writing? (A simple email is often enough.)

LESSON NINE:

HAVE THE CONVERSATION YOU'RE MOST AVOIDING

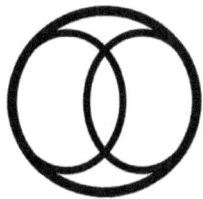

The conversation you're most avoiding is the one you most need to have.

Lesson Nine

In our elevator at work, there were TV screens that gave the weather, quick snippets of news headlines, and the occasional quote. One day in a very grumpy and overwhelmed mood on my way up to the office, I looked up and read, "The conversation you're avoiding is the one you most need to have." Ugh. Sucker punch, right to the face.

To set the stage, I was hard-wired to avoid confrontation like the plague. A friend of mine and I once escaped out the bedroom window of my college apartment to avoid having to walk through a room where two of my roommates were fighting. Conflict and I were not friends then, and that proved no different in my career for many years.

Back to that day in the elevator. I had hired someone on my team who, on paper, had a stellar degree from one of the top universities in the world and who was a very pleasant person. The problem was that she was horrible at her job. I was working like crazy yet took as much time as I could to try and help her get up the learning curve. When I found errors or realized things weren't coming together well, I tried to give supportive feedback. Being highly resistant to hurting people or making them feel bad, I'm sure I probably wasn't as direct as I could have been at times, but I also couldn't hide all the mark-ups and revisions I was spending an extensive amount of time on as we tried to help her learn the job.

We were under a really big crunch with many deliverables all due around the same time. I had no choice but to assign her a project and hope for the best because there wasn't much time for error. Unfortunately, the work she handed in needed to be completely redone. I had to pull an all-nighter to get things turned around in time and out the door to the client.

As soon as she opened what I sent to the client, her heart must have sunk. She emailed me saying she saw how much I redid and asked to talk. I was so tired from the all-nighter and under the gun for all the other things that still needed to get out that I avoided her all day. I had, however, exhaustedly sent her version and the one I redid for the client to my boss simply saying to him: not okay.

At the end of the day, my boss stopped by my office and said he saw what I sent. We had a conversation about her overall performance and what appeared to be a profound lack of fit. She was a great person, and we all really liked her, yet no matter what we tried, things just weren't clicking into place. It was time to talk to her about her fit with the company. Cue me wanting to climb out the window again only this time from the seventh floor up. I said I would; I just needed to get through the next few days. He encouraged me instead to rip the Band-Aid and do it sooner rather than later. My stomach was in knots thinking about how bad she must have felt and how little I wanted to hurt her.

So, when the elevator of enlightenment flashed that message the next morning on my way up, I knew exactly what conversation I was avoiding, and exactly the one I needed to have. In the end, as scary as it was for her to realize she needed to look for a new job, I think it was a relief for her to have a more candid and raw conversation. She'd been sitting there feeling horrible, and after hearing that, I felt horrible too. No one likes to feel like they're struggling, and when they're also trying to figure out where they stand, it's a lot more stressful.

It taught me a good lesson, that leaving people waiting because I want to avoid something is actually crueler and more hurtful than just stepping up and being direct. Now when I realize I'm avoiding talking to someone about something, I know that's the conversation I probably most need to have.

Next time you realize there's a conversation you don't want to have, it's probably worth considering the costs of not having it. It's also worth questioning what you might gain if you did.

Questions to Consider:

Is there a conversation you're avoiding?

How do you think you would feel on the other side of having that conversation?

LESSON TEN:

ACTIONS SPEAK LOUDER THAN WORDS

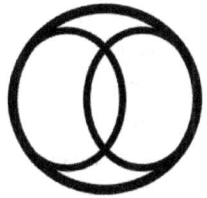

Identifying discrepancies between what someone says and what they do can help navigate tricky situations with more clarity.

Lesson Ten

It's easy to want to believe the best in people or that they're operating from a place of good intent, yet especially in business, people may have different motivations, so it's crucial to pay attention to make sure what someone says and does are matching up.

I am a trusting person. For better or worse, I enter situations believing that people will behave within a reasonable margin of error from how I would, until proven otherwise. I want that kind of consideration extended to me, so I offer it to others. The trust is yours to lose. Unfortunately, I haven't always been great about reading the signs, and I've gotten burned a few too many times. It's made me feel frustrated and angry at myself that I didn't see it coming better and that I didn't stand up for myself or remove myself from the situation sooner.

Examples of how this has shown up include:

- Someone committing to help share in a workload, but then leaving it all to me at the last minute.

- Someone mutually agreeing where I can lead or co-lead something and then talking over me, interrupting, or generally undermining me in front of other people.

There are more examples, but generally speaking, someone has told me one thing, and then either left me holding the bag or they've failed to come through on something they've committed to. It feels awful when it happens, and it's not always easy to navigate addressing it, especially if that person is more senior.

After years of minimizing when people did this, or making it "okay" for them, while not so secretly raging with anger inside, what I've learned is that the most important thing is to catch it when it's happening and get really clear when there's been a breach between what someone said and what they did.

The first clue for me is that anger. If I'm getting upset because of what someone else is or isn't doing, I try to take a time-out to go back through the expectations that we established to see if their actions match up with what was agreed upon. The sooner I see it and acknowledge it to myself, the sooner I can do something about it.

Catching a discrepancy between what someone said they would do and what they actually did as soon as possible is the first step, but I have also learned to be more proactive in addressing things directly with people. Whether it's asking for clarity before jumping to conclusions or expressing my disappointment with something, it's never easy to confront the situation. However, if I don't, the anger I feel for not standing up for myself is on par with the frustration and anger

I feel for them having done what had upset me in the first place.

As an example, one time I was left doing more work because someone didn't do what he had agreed to. The deadline was nearing, and I realized he had not done his part yet. I checked my notes and went to confirm my understanding of the division of labor with him. Despite what was in my notes, he immediately denied that he had agreed to do that portion and launched into a diatribe about how busy he was. Something he had a reputation for doing.

He was more senior than me, so I agreed to handle things even though it really put my back against the wall. From there out, if we were put together on projects, I'd ask to manage the timeline so I could set things up with more wiggle room and include ownership of things. Then I'd circulate it in writing, so we all had it as a reference. I also "over-communicated" by sending frequent reminders about when things were due, who they were assigned to, and copied other people when appropriate. It helped prevent me from getting stuck with another all-nighter.

It can be really confusing when someone says one thing, but then does something different. For a long time, my default was to question myself instead of them. Maybe I misunderstood. I didn't want them to be wrong. It was "easier" for me to be wrong, so I didn't need to confront them about anything. Yet when someone consistently says one thing and does another, it can be very damaging to us if left unchecked.

People look to us to teach them how we want to be treated. It's bad enough when someone doesn't follow through on what they've committed to, but it's made worse when we ignore or enable it. We should go into things with an open mind and optimistic sense of mutual respect, yet always keep an eye on how consistent someone's words and actions are and make sure we're taking care of ourselves.

Questions to Consider:

Are there any places at work where you think someone's actions and words don't match up?

If it impacts you, is there an opportunity for you to ask a clarifying question about what might be going on? (Hint: the next lesson might help.)

Professionaling Is Hard

LESSON ELEVEN:

DON'T TAKE THINGS PERSONALLY

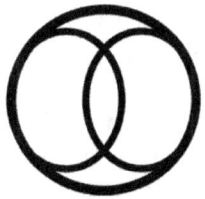

Regardless of what someone is bringing to a situation, it helps to remain neutral and not take anything personally.

Lesson Eleven

It is really hard not to read into things or jump to conclusions when someone says or does something that seems aggressive or off-putting. However, at the end of the day, we can only ever truly know our own intentions, not the intentions of others. When tensions rise or things rub me the wrong way, I try to remind myself that I don't know what's going on with them and not to take it personally. It's not easy, but it helps me stay focused on what's important to me rather than going off-course by reacting to them.

Admittedly, I struggle with this in many facets of my life, so it's something I try to remember every time I realize I'm telling myself a narrative about what's happening with someone else. The simple truth is that people have things going on in their lives that have absolutely nothing to do with me; I just happen to be in front of them.

One time I was in a meeting, and I could feel my defenses rising rapidly. A woman who was there was being short and dismissive toward me. I was convinced she was out for blood and plotting my professional demise behind my back. I started making slightly aggressive comments back to her. "Take that," I was thinking in my head. She wasn't going to get the best of me.

After the meeting, a colleague stopped by my office and said, "what was that?" I instantly launched into a rant, "I know! She was attacking me, what WAS that?!" I saw my colleague's face shift, and I knew something was off. He said he was referring to MY hostility. Why was I being so standoffish to someone whose dog just passed away? Ouch. I totally misread the situation and ended up looking like a total jerk.

While it sounds harsh at first, people simply don't care about us or think about us as much as we care about and think about ourselves. Reading into something or making assumptions about what a person is intending toward us is likely over assigning our importance to them. At the end of the day, we are all hardwired to consider ourselves first so anything we try too hard to infer about another person's intentions is likely more than a few degrees off.

It's also worth noting that while I am a believer that what someone thinks of me is none of my business, at work, what my boss, colleagues, and clients think of me actually matters greatly. I must maintain certain standards and get along well with others. If I make too many assumptions and take things too personally, I'll get distracted and not show up as fully as I need to. There is a balance to strike between being self-aware and emotionally intelligent about what's happening around me with others and remaining true to myself.

If their behavior is too egregious, I know I need to have a conversation with someone. If it's not, and I might be taking it too personally, I try to check myself before reacting.

Clues you might be taking something personally:

- You feel defensive and assume someone is being aggressive or dismissive toward you.

- You're ruminating about what you think someone's intentions are.

Questions to ask yourself:

- Can you know for sure this is about you, or is it possible something else is going on in their world?

- Is this consistent or inconsistent with their usual behavior toward you?

- Do they treat other people similarly?

Based on the answers to those questions I can generally determine if I need to try to remain neutral and give the benefit of the doubt or if something is bubbling up and worthy of monitoring or confronting.

In order to be as effective as we can be at work, it's really important to check in with ourselves when we find we're taking something personally or creating a narrative about what someone is thinking about us. As hard as it can be to shrug things off or not assume someone's intent, things usually work out much better when we give someone the benefit of the doubt and try not to take things personally.

Questions to Consider:

Are there any situations at work where you might have taken something personally that may not have been intended that way?

How might you handle it differently in the future?

Professionaling Is Hard

LESSON TWELVE:

SPEAK UP AND CALL ON OTHERS

*It's important to be heard and invite others
into the conversation.*

Lesson Twelve

Learning how to speak up in a group situation at work can be intimidating when we are starting out or new to a position, yet it is such a critical skill. We are there because we have something to offer, so we should. It also helps when a senior person can invite people into the conversation so more voices are heard.

I will never forget sitting around a boardroom table with the CEO and the Chief Scientific Officer of a company alongside my boss, who had about 25-30 years more experience professionally. I kept looking around me because I felt so deeply out of place. I was nervous and unsure of how to act or what to do... who let me in this room anyway? I'm just a kid. Yikes!

They had a new technology they were working on, and we were hired to help them navigate some tough questions. Before the meeting, my boss had shared a lot about their circumstances, and I had listened in on a few calls, so I felt like I had a basic understanding of things. I had also read a lot about what they were doing and had done some background research on certain considerations. But was I an expert who knew what they should do - heck no.

Sitting in that room that day, I felt deeply nervous out of the gate, yet the more the conversation picked up, the more things started to click. I didn't get all of it, but I had some questions and thought I was piecing things together. It must have been written on my face because at some point my boss asked if I had something to share. I'm fairly confident I turned bright red, and I know I wanted to slide off my chair to hide under the table. I said something to the effect of "no, I'm just listening."

After we left the meeting, I asked some of the questions that I'd been considering, hoping she'd be impressed – yet boy, oh boy, she was not happy with me. She said if I'm sitting in a room like that, it's because I earned that seat, I'm getting paid to sit in it, and people expect me to participate, so I better learn to speak up. She also said that people want me to win. They want young people to offer their perspective, so I need to start engaging when I have something to offer.

Coming from such a successful, respected woman, I took it to heart. As much as it was hard, I learned to find a way of finding my spots and contributing to conversations, even if only minimally. I try to be deeply respectful of others, so it took me a while to learn to insert myself tactfully, by offering a very pointed sentence or two. After doing that more and more, in time it became easier.

As I've progressed in my career, I've tried to pass this on to younger colleagues, women especially. If they report to me, I talk about the value of contributing during our one-on-ones and tell them that I'm going to call on them when we're in a group setting. Then when we are on bigger calls or in bigger meetings, I do make it a point of asking them questions or what they think to make sure that they have the floor. After doing this a few times, these people organically begin speaking up more often in group situations.

The more we flex those muscles, the more we can use them. Yet it really does help to have someone who believes in you and creates an environment where you're called on and encouraged to speak up. If you're looking for more opportunities to participate, ask a manager or colleague who is more vocal if they could ask your opinion or if you have anything to add next time you're in a group meeting or on a group call. If you're used to participating a lot, look around and see if there are other people who might be included in the conversation more often and check in with them to see if they might like more airtime.

Being heard at work matters greatly to advancement and building relationships. You're there because you earned the seat, and people deserve the benefit of your perspective.

Questions to Consider:

Looking around the room in your group meetings:

Are there opportunities for you to chime in that would be appropriate?

If you're not comfortable interjecting yourself, is there a manager or someone you could ask in advance to call on you?

If you're in a position where you speak often, are there other people you could begin to call on to be sure their voices are heard?

Professionaling Is Hard

Section Three: The

Seemingly Contradictory

The next series of lessons at first seem to be oppositional or contradictory with one another, but in truth they present options along a greater continuum. It starts with a lesson about paradoxical thinking or holding the space for many things to be true, and then the lessons that follow provide examples. The paradoxes I talk about have taught me to:

- Not waste so much time trying to get something from good to great - and - invest more time in synthesizing something down to its most potent form.

- Embrace a sense of urgency and timeliness (aka hustle) – and – know when to slow it down to build trust and anticipation.

- Be more inclusive and less inclined to do things solo – and – take credit for work.

- Say no when needed – and – enjoy the power of saying I don't know – and – take more risks by saying yes.

LESSON THIRTEEN:

THE BEAUTY IN PARADOXICAL THINKING

Allowing space for more than one thing to be "right" is often what is most true.

Lesson Thirteen

Like many of us, I grew up in a world that preferred binary thinking over leaving any room for middle ground. Things were right or wrong, yes or no, in or out. In time, I have realized that rarely in life is anything all one way or another. More often than not, the truth exists somewhere in between. Learning to be aware of that, much less manage it, is no easy feat, but trying to live from a place of paradox where both/and is most often the truest answer has been incredibly helpful.

Earlier in my career, I felt much more strongly about the rightness of things and the injustices associated with them. When I was working incredibly long hours and not getting any breaks, support, or extra compensation for it, I felt very sure that it was wrong. They were wrong for not seeing how much I was sacrificing and for not offering any help or throwing me a bone. I spent a lot of time angry and frustrated that they weren't seeing what I thought was an injustice.

In the years since then, I've learned that it's not that simple, and I held plenty of responsibility for my circumstances. Had I been less inclined to see things so right and wrong, maybe I would have had the perspective to say yes, things are both way out of balance AND I'm the only one who's seeing it and can do something about it. I wish I had known better how to add the second half of a sentence. If I had, I could have felt more power in the situation instead of feeling a victim of circumstance. Adding that second half didn't change that I didn't agree with what they were doing or make it okay, but it would have put me in a better position to do something about it.

Another example is the many times in my career when I was working in jobs less because I was in love with that company or position and more because it was a means to an end while I was hoping to be on my way to something else. At times I would be very frustrated or angry at the job or the people I was working with, yet I would try to remind myself that it was what I was choosing. It was both a very frustrating situation and it was a means to an end, one I was grateful to have so I could prioritize other things too, even though I did occasionally reserve the right to throw myself on the floor and pout like a toddler.

Learning how to hold the space for more than one thing to be true has helped me reclaim power and feel more grateful. Next time you find yourself frustrated, question if you're holding onto something being 'right' or only one way and see if you might be able to add an 'and' to the end of the sentence. Perhaps more than one thing is true, and you may find yourself feeling more powerful and in a much better position to navigate things.

Questions to Consider:

Is there a situation you're frustrated with where it might benefit to add an 'and' to the end of the sentence?

How might things shift if the second half were there?

Paradox 1:

Don't Let Perfect Be the Enemy of Good

AND

If I Had More Time, I Would Have Written Less

The next two lessons are about managing time and being as effective as possible.

- Don't Let Perfect Be the Enemy of Good helps assess when we're spending too much time on something, possibly in vain.

- If I Had More Time, I Would've Written Less explores how distilling a message down to its most powerful form usually isn't a quick process, but is often worth it.

Professionaling Is Hard

LESSON FOURTEEN:

DON'T LET PERFECT BE THE ENEMY OF GOOD

Sometimes good is good enough – striving for 'perfect' prevents us from accomplishing more.

Lesson Fourteen

It's so tempting to want to get everything right, perfectly, wonderfully right. Yet how often is "right" an actual thing versus something subjective that we spend way too much time fussing over when we could be doing more and getting more accomplished? Learning the line between perfect and good and when good is acceptable is a major lesson in being more effective.

I like doing things well. If I'm doing it, I want it done to a level I'm proud of. I don't like people to see my work before it's ready unless there are broad disclaimers everywhere that it's in draft form. When the recipient of something I'm preparing first opens or receives it, I want them to be able to focus on what's important, not distracted by a mistake or an error. I may or may not be a recovering perfectionist.

So, it was far later than I wish it had been when I first heard the phase by Voltaire – "don't let perfect be the enemy of good." Wait, you mean all that time and effort spent trying to get something to perfect may have been wasted because good enough would have done the job? No one would have noticed those tiny details that took an exhaustive amount of time?

I was already familiar with the rule of 80/20 that generally speaking 20% of something takes up 80%

of the effort or resources and it immediately reminded me of that. It made me question how I might be able to shift my line of what I considered "done" and get more time to do more things. Was that last push of effort what was really going to make or break something, or was I just moving boxes around on a screen fixating on a "perfect" that's ultimately subjective?

I'm still learning to lessen my expectations and find wherever that elusive line between good and perfect is, but I have learned to live with a lot more imperfection. And unsurprisingly, I can't honestly say that I've gotten feedback that the quality of my work dropped. If anything, I think it's helped me to focus more on getting what matters right and worrying less about the other stuff. Some things do require a level of precision, yet learning what those are and becoming more flexible in other places is a great way to manage time and get more done.

The next time you've edited the same line 20 times or moved and removed something from 15 places, it's worth considering if you're letting perfect be the enemy of good. Especially if good is good enough, learn to set and appreciate those lines. Asking your manager or someone with many years of experience how they establish where that line is might also provide you with some insight.

Questions to Consider:

Is there an area in your work where you might be able to spend a little less time but get comparable results?

What else might you be able to do if you spent less time on that?

LESSON FIFTEEN:

IF I HAD MORE TIME, I WOULD'VE WRITTEN LESS

Convey the message in as few words as possible.

Lesson Fifteen

First attributed to French mathematician and philosopher Blaise Pascal, the saying "if I had more time, I would've written less" truly captures the battle that is achieving conciseness. While it takes more work to crisply articulate what matters, it's the best way of being understood and bringing people along with you.

This is an inspiration for why this book is not ten times longer than it is. Why use 100 words when ten would make the point? Say less, mean more. It's that simple and yet it really isn't. To get to the point, one must process, analyze, synthesize, and distill to convey the shortest, most cogent summary.

It became my motto when I was working in market research, and using that process as an example, illustrates the concept beautifully. For my job, I would conduct interviews with people, those interviews would be recorded and turned into transcripts. I would read those transcripts and analyze them to find patterns in responses for each question that was asked. Then I would take those patterns and findings from my notes and translate them into slides that reported the findings. I would do this for every question that was asked in an interview, slide by painful slide.

Once a thorough reporting of all the findings was complete, I would go back and pull together a slide or two of key findings to help summarize things. After that, I would go back to the client's business objectives and consider those in relationship with what the findings were so I could create a one-slide executive summary. This summary told the client exactly what they needed to know from the research as crisply and directly as possible. Dozens of hours of interviews and labor to boil it down to a handful of meaningful sentences.

This was clearly in the days before AI cut this process down to a fraction of the human-required work that I just listed, but the point is - sometimes you must distill a large amount of information down multiple times before you can get to the most poignant and direct statements. And yet, that's what helps other people understand things more quickly and easily. Learning how to say less and mean more is an invaluable skill.

Questions to Consider:

Are there things you write that could be more powerful or actionable if you took extra time to make the message clearer?

If you need an answer to something, how can you make the question obvious and easy to understand?

Paradox 1: Summary

It can be really challenging to know how much time to spend on something and when good enough is enough. In some ways it is a skill developed over time, but it's something we can play with to expedite that learning.

Thinking of all the work we have at hand, there are likely some safe places to play with letting go of locking up every single detail or nit-picking something arbitrary. Identifying those opportunities and seeing what happens when we hit send instead of fussing can be a fairly low-risk way of getting some time back. If no one notices, great. If someone comments, you can always take responsibility and adjust next time.

It's also worth exploring where you might want to invest more time distilling your message down so that when it is conveyed, it is as crisp and as powerful as it can be. Cutting through the noise and confusion so that something is immediately understandable is a true gift to others and a service to us as well. Summarizing points into bullets, ending an email with a strong sentence about what needs to be answered or addressed are some ways of playing with this concept.

While spending less time on "perfect" and more time on being concise may seem conflicting, both are in service of using time to your advantage and getting things done as effectively as possible.

Paradox 2:

Hustle Matters

AND

Take a Pause

The next two lessons focus on urgency and timeliness (also known as (aka): hustle) and slowing things down.

- Hustle Matters is all about the near, and long-term benefits of demonstrating a sense of urgency and timeliness for getting things done.

- Take a Pause describes the positives associated with learning to slow things down a little bit and speak with intention.

Professionaling Is Hard

LESSON SIXTEEN:

HUSTLE MATTERS

*Demonstrating a solid work ethic creates
meaningful and enduring impressions.*

Lesson Sixteen

When someone shows up and hustles to get things done and puts their all into what they're doing, they can not only be proud of themselves, but more than likely get noticed and crack open new doors along the way.

I have no idea where I'd be if I didn't have a sense of urgency and timeliness to get things done, otherwise known as "hustle." For context, I may or may not have a history of speeding, and I may or may not have gotten a speeding ticket while listening to Ludacris' song "Move Bitch Get Out Da Way." If I could count the number of times I've sat in traffic or navigated busy highways with people seemingly dillydallying around while I beg-screamed that they just needed to get a sense of urgency, I'd be a very wealthy woman. (Worth noting, I keep my road antics to a self-contained simmer and not a full-blown rage.)

This sense of GET THERE, MAKE IT HAPPEN is ingrained in me. I always wish there were more hours in a day, and I'm all for working smarter, not harder, but even when I find efficiencies, that just creates more space to DO things. I don't sit still well, and that's served me well in my career.

Even as a college student, my hustle helped me secure a better position at a new bakery that was just opening. I was one of their first hires, and despite being younger than many other people, I was made the manager of the front-end. I'd always show up for work a little early, and if I was on the clock, I was doing something that supported the business. If it was rush hour, I was helping direct the flow and make sure things were running well, and I'd jump in wherever needed. If it was quiet, I was cleaning, organizing, and doing things to help keep it all running well. It didn't go unnoticed, and I appreciated the extra responsibility of being a manager.

That sentiment carried over into my more professional endeavors too. I've tended to opt for employers and situations where there was less bureaucracy and structure so I could demonstrate my work ethic and climb more quickly. I earned a VP title at thirty and was in the C-suite by my early forties. One thing that's helped give me the confidence to take risks and go for big things is knowing that I'm not afraid to work hard and that there are now many people along the way who I've demonstrated that to as well.

That hustle is what's opened several doors and brought many opportunities from people I've worked with in the past who've wanted me to be a part of what they're doing. While I'm grateful to them for seeing and appreciating that, I'm also proud of myself that I've consistently shown up and given things my all.

I feel a sense of fulfillment that comes from accomplishing things and making progress. And I've found that having a healthy sense of hustle can impress people and create new opportunities. Because you just never know who's watching and what doors a little urgency and timeliness might open up for you now, or down the road.

Question to Consider:

Is there something you could do or (reasonably) take on that would demonstrate initiative beyond what you're already doing, which would save someone else time and/or get good visibility?

A bite-sized example: someone asks for a status update every Monday morning – instead of waiting for the request to come in, schedule it on your calendar and start proactively sending it in advance. It's something you need to do anyway, but you're saving them the work of having to ask for it. (Note: be honest with yourself about your capacity and don't take on anything too big, or it could backfire and have negative consequences.)

LESSON SEVENTEEN:

TAKE A PAUSE

*Pausing before a response conveys
consideration and can pull people in.*

Lesson Seventeen

Sometimes, rather than rushing in with a quick response, it's better to take a moment to find the right response. The need to fire back a fast reply during a live interaction can feel anxiety-producing to say the least, but often, a better approach is to breathe and allow even a few seconds of time to process things more thoroughly before responding.

A colleague of mine was a fiercely intelligent, hard-working, kind human. We got along incredibly well and were very supportive of one another. We were in client services and often worked on projects together.

When we needed to have calls to kick-off a new project, or other important client interaction, we would gather in the conference room or in someone's office and hop on a conference line (back in the pre-Zoom dark ages). We'd start discussing things with the client, and from time to time things would get more intense or more tense in general. As a high-energy lady from the East Coast, my natural tendency was to respond immediately and address things as quickly as I could possibly get the words out of my mouth. My inner angst told me that leaving any dead airtime was an opportunity for them to doubt that I knew what I was talking about or to question my capabilities.

My Minnesota-native colleague, on the other hand, was never afraid of a pregnant pause on these calls, causing some heart palpitations on my part. I'll never forget the first time he was asked something by a client on one of our group calls, and he paused... for... what... seemed... like... forever... before... he... finally... responded. In all those seconds, I recall panicking, wondering if he didn't know the answer, was making something up, was asleep with his eyes open, or was ordering lunch in his mind - desperately wanting to jump in and answer for him - my mind and my pulse were racing. I was reeling with ruminations about what the client might be thinking about me if I let that much time lapse before I responded.

In reality, he paused for maybe 7-10 seconds, but it felt like a lifetime. After one of these panic-inducing pause calls, a senior colleague of ours complimented him on this exact skill. She said it's easy to want to rush in with an answer sometimes, but it shows deeper consideration when you take a second to contemplate something before diving in with a response because people know you've thought through what you said. Hmmm. No kidding.

It taught me the value of slowing things down and allowing time for contemplation so everyone would get the best and highest response.

I admit I still can't leave dead air for too long so what I have taught myself to do instead is to initially respond by indicating I am taking a beat to think about something. Phrases like:

- "That's a great question; let me think about that for a moment."

- "Great point; let me mentally tease that out for a second."

- "Interesting, I need to think about that one for a minute."

- "I'm processing; let me consider that quickly before I respond."

Those phrases help me accomplish the goal of giving myself a pause to consider something while also making sure someone knows I'm on top of it.

As if that weren't enough already, another benefit of learning to take a pause before diving in is that it causes people to lean in. We're hard-wired to keep conversations flowing, and when someone pauses, it somehow builds anticipation and naturally causes us to lean in to hear what is about to be said. What a powerful tool to keep in mind.

People trust what's being shared when they know someone has taken time to think things through. Learning from him that taking a pause can demonstrate confidence and consideration is one of the best lessons I've received along the way.

Question to Consider:

Are there times when it might be beneficial to slow things down a bit and pause before responding?

Paradox 2: Summary

Showing a sense of hustle and slowing things down to take a pause can seem very much at odds with one another. However, both have an important role in shaping how people consider our contributions.

People who demonstrate a sense of urgency to get things done in a timely way are deemed incredibly valuable to most, if not all, leaders. Finding small but visible ways of showing the people we want to impress and continue to work with that we have hustle is an important key to forming strong relationships at work.

There are also times when learning to take a pause before diving in shows thoughtfulness, consideration, and builds confidence in what we say. All of which is critical to building trust and lasting connections.

Learning to bring both a sense of hustle and an ability to slow things down and demonstrate confident consideration are powerful tools that will help you leave positive, lasting impressions.

Paradox 3:

Don't Go It Alone

AND

Take Credit for Your Work

The next two lessons are about finding people to surround yourself with along the journey instead of doing it all on your own, and ensuring we are given credit when it is due.

- Don't Go It Alone discusses the importance of not feeling like we have to do everything on our own and the benefits of finding other people who have skills we lack.

- Take Credit for Your Work is about ensuring that when we work with others, our contributions are acknowledged when they should be.

Professionaling Is Hard

LESSON EIGHTEEN:

DON'T GO IT ALONE

"If you want to go fast, go alone, if you want to go far, go together."- African Proverb

Lesson Eighteen

While it's tempting and may seem easier to muscle through and maintain control over everything, we're all human, and everyone has their limits. If we want to grow and reach our full potential, we simply can't go it totally alone. Just as there are only so many hours in a day, there's only so much we can know, and be good at, and do on our own.

As a little girl, I grew up with an entrepreneurial father who I looked up to in immeasurable ways. One of the things I remember him saying frequently was "partners are for dancing, not business." As a solopreneur for many years of his career, I understood why he felt this way. Yet as time has gone on, I think he's come to see the value of having more people around and not going it alone. Looking back, he wonders about the kind of growth he could have achieved and how far he could have gone if he had brought more people in around him sooner.

As a woman who's tried and failed at getting many of her own business ideas into the world, I've come to realize that a large part of my inability to get things fully launched is that I tried too hard to do it all by myself instead of bringing more people into the fold to help me.

One of my dreams was to start a company that would raise awareness and funding for organizations supporting patients by creating videos of inspirational people living with those conditions. For years I interviewed patients to get their stories for market research purposes. There were so many times that I left those conversations utterly blown away by what someone dealt with and managed on a day-to-day basis. How they had what can only be called an enlightened perspective on life and an empowered way of moving through the world always left me humbled and beyond inspired. All I wanted in the world was to put those same people in the position of being able to help other people like them and hopefully having even a little bit of all their amazingness reflected back at them.

There were many starts and stops in trying to create that business over eight years. I formed a company, took courses on video editing and other things, reached out to people, recorded interviews, made videos, I even had a patent issued related to the idea. I was able to get things to certain points, but I always blinked and put it down. I know a large part of why I was never fully able to get it launched and realize that dream is because I felt I had to know everything and do it all on my own. In hindsight, I can see that going it alone is what stopped it from actually going.

While I agree partnerships can add degrees of complication, on a more practical level, whether we're talking about starting a business or trying to survive in a new job, it's a lonely and longer road if we try to do it all solo. One of the smartest women I ever worked for told me much of her success was due to knowing what her strengths were and surrounding herself with people whose strengths were where her deficits were. We can't all be good at everything, so finding ways of expanding talent and abilities only helps grow what a team is capable of accomplishing.

To that end, if I could go back in time and do it over again, I would have found the courage to approach videographers, producers, social media experts, non-profit leaders, people with skills and expertise that I lacked when I was trying to get things started. I would have put myself out there to see if someone wanted to collaborate with me and build a bigger base of knowledge to get things going. Maybe I would have felt less alone, and it would have felt more doable.

It's easy to want to hide what we don't know or to want to go it alone so it's all in our control. Those things feel easier at first, yet ultimately, they keep us operating from a place of fear and in isolation. While it's a lot harder to take a risk and expose where we need support or to take a leap and bring someone in, it can also be the bridge that opens us to new lands.

Question to Consider:

Is there anything you're struggling with that might be made better by finding someone to partner up with?

LESSON NINETEEN:

TAKE CREDIT FOR YOUR WORK

Get the credit you deserve, find and/or be an
ally in making sure it is allocated properly.

Lesson Nineteen

When we do great work or offer solid contributions, it's essential to learn to take credit for our accomplishments. Other people can be all too eager to swoop in and take credit for things, and if we over-assign credit to the group, our efforts can get lost in the process.

At one point in my career, I was in an environment where the ideas I presented and the work I did would often be credited to male colleagues instead of to me. I remember sitting in rooms brainstorming, coming up with creative solutions, and making some bold recommendations - only to have one of them repeat or reiterate what I said, and get all the credit. It felt like I was invisible, a professional fairy godmother sent in to whisper strategic visions and ideas in their ears so they could look like heroes while no one even knew I was there.

During one of these encounters, I absolutely snapped. When a male colleague was given credit for something I had just suggested, I couldn't hold it in anymore. I very loudly said, "I JUST SAID THAT." I got looked at like I had 15 heads, and clearly, it must be my time of the month. Fortunately, the colleague the credit was assigned to came to see me after the meeting. Once I snapped, he saw what was happening. He apologized for not seeing it sooner and validated my experience. After that, he became a great ally in making sure that if something came from me, the credit would be redirected back to me when others tried to allocate it elsewhere, especially to him.

I'm far from the only person to endure that phenomenon, but that only makes it more infuriating, not less. I feel very lucky that I had a colleague who supported me and helped me learn to take credit for things, but I didn't always, and I know not everyone is so fortunate. With his support I felt more confident in owning my contributions knowing someone had my back.

At another point in my career, when I had a team working for me, I generally phrased things as "we" when I was speaking about what was happening and what was done. Even when it may have been fair to say that I was directly responsible for something or pulled something off, I generally tended to share the credit when speaking with people senior to me or to a broad audience. I'm sure one part of that was my discomfort with the perception that I'm boasting or bragging, and another part was wanting to make sure that my team was seen in a favorable light and given the credit they were due.

It's that first part though, the part of me that doesn't want to be perceived in a certain way, that's proven problematic. After I had left that job where I managed a team I appreciated and was deeply proud of, I was interviewing for something and consistently used the phrase "we" when responding about accomplishments and experiences. It was a habit leftover from being in that role with that team, but the person interviewing me stopped midway and said, "I'm sorry, you keep saying 'we', I'm having a hard time understanding what you actually did and were responsible for."

He said it in a slightly hostile way, so I knew he was irritated. I tried to explain how as the manager of such a high-performing team I was used to all of us sharing in our successes. Our mentality was "we" verses "I". I don't think it was appreciated. I tried to reframe my responses and demonstrate what I personally was capable of; however, the rest of the interview felt terse, and he ended the conversation early.

I didn't get the job, and I'm entirely okay with that. I don't particularly want to work with people who don't value teamwork in the same way. Yet it did teach me that I need to get more comfortable speaking about my accomplishments - both as a team, and individually. To take credit for what I've done and all I've achieved without hiding behind a group.

Learning to confidently take credit for the work we do is an important step in being recognized and valued for what we bring to the table. We should tell the truth about what we've done, and when possible, find allies and be allies to others so we can back each other up and reinforce assigning credit where it belongs.

Questions to Consider:

If you're missing out on opportunities to have your contributions or work recognized, are there any allies you might be able to enlist to help you get noticed?

Who might support you in getting credit for your contributions?

Are there people on your team or who you work with whose voices may not be heard or whose contributions might not be getting recognized?

How could you help support other people in getting credit where it's due?

Paradox 3: Summary

Feeling alone or like we need to tackle everything on our own can hinder us from realizing our potential. It is also critical to ensure that when we're working with others, credit is allocated appropriately.

As much as taking the lead or maintaining total control over a project or situation may feel satisfying for a while, the simple truth is that we can be stronger and go further when we work together. Even individuals like Beyoncé, Oprah, and Taylor Swift, who appear omnipotent and endlessly talented, are not proficient at everything. They have teams of people with strengths that complement their own, enabling them to excel in their areas of expertise. It's also more fun and less lonely when we have company along for the ride.

Getting credit for the hard work we put in is critical to so many things. It can seem easy and maybe even comfortable to shrug off someone else getting the nod for our contributions. However, when it comes to promotions, bonuses, or desirable assignments, having been acknowledged for your efforts undoubtedly matters.

We shouldn't go it alone, and we must ensure that we know how to receive the appropriate credit for our contributions.

Paradox 4:

No Is a Full Sentence

AND

Sometimes the Best Thing to Say Is – I Don't Know

AND

Say Yes, Take More Risks

The last three lessons are about learning when to say no, I don't know, and when to embrace risk and say yes!

- No Is a Full Sentence offers perspective about knowing when to draw lines and set limits.

- Sometimes the Best Thing to Say Is – I Don't Know embraces the magic that happens when we tell the truth about not knowing something and build trust when we follow up with the answer.

- Say Yes, Take More Risks asks us to tap into what we love and be bold when considering our choices.

Professionaling Is Hard

LESSON TWENTY:

NO IS A FULL SENTENCE

Learn to say no.

Lesson Twenty

It's really tempting to be a yes person at work. It seems the obvious way to get the opportunities, the experiences, and the rewards of a job well done. In many ways, it is what's required and puts people ahead, yet like excessive anything, too much yessing can lead to negative consequences. It's important to be aware of when yeses are compromising you and maybe even the work you're doing. Finding a way of pushing back or learning to say no is also important.

There was a point in my career where I wish I knew better how to say no. "It's going to be so fun guys, we can do it, I'll help!" This was what my boss would craftily exclaim to my colleague and me after pulling us away from the projects we were already inundated with, so we could help him scope new work. Initially, my colleague and I would groan from our exhaustion. We just wanted to plow through and get things done, but when the boss calls you in, you go.

Once we were in his office, he'd set the scene, making sure to paint things in a way that made us feel like the clients were in trouble and we were their last hope – only we could save them with the magical powers of our market researching prowess. He'd lure us in with the details of their circumstances, the complicated questions they desperately needed answers to, and importantly, he'd take to the whiteboard to get our minds in gear working out how to construct the right research instrument to solve this imminent threat to their wellbeing. He made us feel like we were superheroes! Sure, we were tired, yes, we definitely had more on our plates than we were capable of doing in the sometimes 80 hours per week we were putting in, but would we let that stop us from helping these fine people in need - of course not! And he'd be right there with us to roll up his sleeves and fight the good fight as our fearless leader right alongside us!

Having agreed to take on the project after this dramatic effort to make us feel supported, my colleague and I would wander back to our offices bolstered by our sense of mission to help - our capes flowing in the gentle wake of heroism flowing behind us. In time, we came to realize his production, that rah-rah WE can do it team, convincing us to take on more than what was reasonable with no extra anything but more work - that was all the "help" we would get from him. Not his time or effort getting things done, not extra resources or compensation, nothing. What he would do, however, is promptly go take naps in his office while we were putting in incredibly long hours to pull off what he got us to foolishly agree to take on.

After this happened more than a couple of times, I started referring to it as Tom Sawyer management. Just as in Mark Twain's novel, after Tom's aunt (management) came down on him (our boss) to get the fence painted (win the new project) he'd use reverse psychology to convince the neighborhood kids (my colleague and me) to trade small trinkets and treasures (our time, energy, and dollar per hour average as salaried employees) for the "privilege" of doing his tedious work because of the joy it would bring them (us). What a load.

I know he was doing his best to motivate us and increase production for the company, but what I wish I'd known then is that the word no is a full sentence. There are definitely times in a career to enthusiastically say yes to taking on big things and putting in a lot of hours, but this was different. I only wish I had known that it was not only okay, but totally appropriate for me to push back when we were being taken advantage of. I wish I had been better able to say no and stand by it.

Fortunately, since then, I've learned something that I use when I'm maxed out and my plate is running over in a way that is unsustainable and someone wants to keep adding until the plate risks breaking. At those times, the best thing I can do is make a list of everything I'm responsible for. Once I've made visual all that I'm managing, I can ask for help prioritizing and rearranging things. Oftentimes that leads to either saying no to something or resetting expectations around when things will happen. When I've done that with colleagues, it enabled us to have more clarity before anything was at risk or I was run into the ground.

If you're like me, there will likely always be times when we catch ourselves feeling the crush of total overwhelm because there is more being asked of us than can reasonably be done in the time given. Remembering that no is a full sentence will give you permission to find the right approach to make sure you're honoring yourself and what you believe is right for you.

Question to Consider:

Consider a time you felt overwhelmed at work, was there an opportunity to list everything going on and review it with someone who could have helped you reprioritize things to take some pressure off?

Professionaling Is Hard

LESSON TWENTY-ONE:

SOMETIMES THE BEST THING TO SAY IS - I DON'T KNOW

Honesty truly is the best policy – admitting you don't know something can have benefits.

Lesson Twenty-One

While it can seem scary at first to expose a lack of knowledge about something, saying you don't know can not only build more trust in the things you do know but allow time to find the right answers and deepen people's respect for you in the process.

It flies in the face of everything I ever felt on the inside. The crushing pressure to be right, to know the answer, to not look stupid, bad, dumb. I am embarrassed to think of how many times, personally and professionally, in order to avoid looking like a fool, I would nod that I knew something when really, I had absolutely no idea at all.

No one wants to look like they don't have all the answers, especially when they're new to a career, a job, a profession. Making a solid impression on colleagues and clients (if applicable) is critical. And while yes, there is some amount of "fake it till you make it" attitude that can be helpful at times, becoming aware of when it is best to own that you don't know something is an incredibly powerful tool that can work to your advantage.

I will never forget the day I had this realization. I was working in client services, later in my 20's than I'd like to admit, at a meeting at a fancy office in Cambridge, MA, a mecca for geniuses worldwide. So, it shocked me when one of our clients, someone who was on the leadership team who it seemed should have known the answer to something when pressed, responded by saying "you know what, I'm not sure about that, let me look into it and get back to you."

Mind blown. Wait, what, that's an option?!

Admittedly, that's a very fancy and professional way of saying "I don't know," but still, it took me a minute to realize, that he just owned the fact that he wasn't sure about something, promised to get the right answer, and everyone was okay with that? As the conversation went on, I also began to realize that it actually had the side benefit of building trust that when he gave responses to other things - I knew he knew what he was talking about and that it was the right answer.

Bam. Mind blown again. Admit you don't know something AND build trust and confidence with others? Whoa.

I quickly learned to adopt this approach into my own way of interacting with people. To this day when I'm not sure about something and the right answer is important, I simply say: "I'm not 100% sure about that, let me look into it and I'll get back to you." It keeps the conversation moving, and it gives me an opportunity to follow up, which sometimes is an added benefit.

There is so much pressure to know things and to be right all the time. It is important when you're getting paid to know things. Yet the ability to admit when you don't know something and commit to getting the right answer can be a powerful tool to help build trust and confidence in the depth of your knowledge and commitment to getting things right for people.

Questions to Consider:

Can you recall a situation where it would have been better to admit not knowing something?

Would there have been any benefits to owning it and later following up with the answer?

LESSON TWENTY-TWO:

SAY YES, TAKE MORE RISKS

Take chances, say yes to what you feel passion for!

Lesson Twenty-Two

Time and again, when I ask successful professionals what they wish they'd known when they were younger or what they'd do if they could do it over again, the responses relate to taking more or bigger risks than they had. Simply put, you'll never know if you don't try.

Early in my career, the woman I was working for was renting an office within her friend's floor of a professional building. The friend who let her use the space was smart, kind, and in love with what he did for a living, and it showed. To this day he remains one of the most successful and one of the most positive people I've met. I'll never forget sitting in his office while he talked to me about the risks he'd taken in his business and career. The words of wisdom he shared were that if you do what you love, the money will follow. That was his secret to success.

It sounded lovely but with heaps of student loan debt that felt like a fantasy world I'd never gain entry into. I wish I had more gumption back then and a better sense of what I loved, but his advice was solid even if learning what I loved only came in whispers along the way.

That job itself was one of those whispers. I was looking for things online and saw a posting for a newly formed consulting group that had a fancy logo and even though the role sounded like a huge stretch for me, I was instantly intrigued. "The firm" was one woman who had recently left a very senior job at a very major international company so she could start her own consulting group. She was a big deal. I was a very small, inexperienced fish hoping to swim in her very deep waters. I thought there was no way she would be interested in me, but the woman who was interning for her (also her babysitter) convinced her I was worth talking to.

When I landed an interview, it felt good to talk to someone that smart and that well-respected doing big important things with so much vigor and passion. It was inspiring, meaningful work, and as much as I wasn't qualified, I wanted in on what she was doing. I was scared, and it felt like a big risk joining a one-woman consulting "group," but I trusted it was the right move, and I'm so glad I swung big and took the chance when she offered me a job.

While I was only there for a year, in the years since then, I have looked back so many times and marveled at how much that role formed and shaped much of my career. I don't even want to imagine where I would be today if I hadn't listened to what felt good and said yes to taking a risk on something I thought I wasn't ready for.

When we pay attention to what lights us up or what resonates with us in a way that feels right, it's important to take the leap. When it comes to saying yes and taking chances on things that seem like a stretch – I know many people who wish they'd taken more risks along the way, and not one single person who wishes they'd taken fewer.

Questions to Consider:

Are there risks you wish you'd taken and didn't?

How, if at all, might you evaluate opportunities differently in the future?

Paradox 4: Summary

Life is full of surprises and challenges. It's important to develop a sense of when it's okay to say no or push back on something, when it's best to own not knowing something, and when to enthusiastically dive in and say yes to something.

Drawing lines, setting limits, and saying no can be really hard, but it also helps us say yes to other things and be more focused on what we have already agreed to. If you're feeling overwhelmed or pinched beyond what's bearable, it might be time to make things visual in a list and get help prioritizing, resetting expectations, or saying no.

Trust is such an important thing to develop with colleagues. When we learn to be bold enough to say we're not sure about something, but we will follow up with the right answer, it puts more faith in what we do know, and it allows us to continue the conversation. Next time you're not sure about something, pause and consider if owning that you don't know is the best option.

Amazing things can happen when we learn to trust our gut and say yes to opportunities that feel aligned with where we want to go. Taking risks always feels a little shaky, but you never know if you don't try. If you're feeling drawn to something, even if it seems bigger than what you're ready for or like it's a bridge too far, stop and ask yourself what your future self of five years from now might tell you to do.

There are rarely perfect answers 100% of the time, so learning how to check in with yourself to see whether you need to say no, I don't know, or yes is an invaluable practice to develop.

Hopefully after reading these lessons, you feel more confident in how to navigate the professional world and empowered to have the career you deserve. What you have to offer is so very valuable, and it all starts with making sure you support and honor yourself.

When things get challenging or you're feeling pinched, remember some of the lessons we went through in the first section of the book that focused on building and reinforcing inner strength:

- You don't have to know everything on day one, you just need to show you can figure it out.

- Don't put too much pressure on one decision (in a lifetime of continually making new ones).

- Identifying and taking one tiny action can free you from being stuck.

- Setting expectations so you can exceed them is a good way to make a great impression.

- Remembering to focus on what we already know helps build confidence when the pressure is on.

Working with others is rewarding and at times can be difficult to maneuver. When you encounter tricky interpersonal dynamics at work, I hope you'll come back to some of the lessons from the second part of the book.

- Mistakes happen, report them quickly with some thought towards possible solutions.

- When feedback is general or not specific enough to be informative, ask for an example.

- Get promises or commitments in writing to ensure there is a documented mutual understanding.

- The conversation you're most avoiding is the one you most need to have.

- Identifying discrepancies between what someone says and what they do can help navigate tricky situations with more clarity.

- Regardless of what someone is bringing to a situation, it helps to remain neutral and not take anything personally.

- It's important to be heard and invite others into the conversation.

Professionaling involves a lot of uncertainty. Finding the best answer given the circumstances before us is all we can really do. Hopefully the last section of the book helped open up options to exploring more than one pathway to handling something and can be used as a resource to turn to again and again.

- Allowing space for more than one thing to be "right" is often what is most true.

- Sometimes good is good enough - striving for "perfect" prevents us from accomplishing more.

- Convey the message in as few words as possible.

- Demonstrating a solid work ethic creates meaningful and enduring impressions.

- Pausing before a response conveys consideration and can pull people in.

- "If you want to go fast, go alone, if you want to go far, go together." - African Proverb

- Get the credit you deserve, find and/or be an ally in making sure it is allocated properly.

- Learn to say no.

- Honesty truly is the best policy - admitting you don't know something can have benefits.

- Take chances, say yes to what you feel passion for!

When you encounter the inevitable bumps or issues at work, I hope you'll remember what I shared here and find encouragement for how to handle things. This book will be here for you to come back to anytime. I hope that by sharing the lessons I've learned moving through the professional world things will be even a little easier for you as you advance in your own career.

You already know more than you think you do. You offer tremendous value to the world, and you are so very worthy of creating a career and life of your dreams. Go get it!

Acknowledgements

Mom, thank you for encouraging my lifelong love of reading and books, among so very many things. Thank you also for still editing for me, and for still trying to get me to stop using run on sentences.

Boomy, your work ethic and ability to find levity are among the gifts I'm most grateful to have grown up around. Thank you for showing me the way.

Gratitude beyond measure to my squad of believers: Alli, Cari, Christina, Jasmine, Lisa, and Lynn.

Nora, Daniel, Colin, Noah, and Aidan thank you for inspiring me to want to be better and offer all that I can. I can't wait to watch all that you each do.

Mairelisa, thank you for your encouragement and thoughtful perspective. Your success is inevitable.

I am endlessly grateful to all the colleagues, bosses, and employers I've had along the way for all the opportunities to grow and experiences gained.

My love, thank you.

Professionaling Is Hard

Kristin is a C-level executive with over 20 years working in the healthcare and life sciences industries. She is a patent holder and peer-reviewed journal author who has played a foundational role at several startup companies and spent many years in client services as a consultant and market researcher. All of these experiences supplied her with many, many lessons she only wishes she'd learned sooner.

Her mission is to help empower more people to find joy at work and live full, extraordinary lives. She holds degrees from The University of New Hampshire and Boston University. When not professionaling, Kristin loves to spend time being active outside and connecting with the people she loves.